California
(on the Someș)

Ruxandra Cesereanu

California
(on the Someș)

Translated from Romanian by
Adam J. Sorkin and Ruxandra Cesereanu

BLACK
WIDOW
PRESS

Boston

Black Widow Press is an imprint of Commonwealth Books, Inc., Boston, MA. Distributed to the trade by NBN (National Book Network) throughout North America, Canada, and the U.K. All Black Widow Press books are printed on acid-free paper, and glued into bindings. Black Widow Press and its logo are registered trademarks of Commonwealth Books, Inc.

Joseph S. Phillips and Susan J. Wood, Ph.D., Publishers
www.blackwidowpress.com

Cover photograph by Yoshiro Sakamoto
Interior art: Views of the Someş, photographs by Yoshiro Sakamoto
Author photo by Călina Bora
Design & production: Kerrie L. Kemperman

ISBN-13: 978-1-7371603-4-2

Printed in the United States
10 9 8 7 6 5 4 3 2 1

Acknowledgments

Sections from *California (on the Someș)* appeared previously in the following literary journals: *Poem [UK]*, *Catamaran*, *New Poetry in Translation*, and *Talisman*.

Translator's Foreword

–Adam J. Sorkin

Translators can work very skillfully limiting themselves to only the words of the original text, but as someone who has always collaborated with a native speaker of Romanian for the nuances of language and the suggestive and allusive qualities of the poet's diction, I've often found the author my best resource to evoke as much as possible the qualities, meanings and associations intended. In the case of Ruxandra Cesereanu, whom I have known since we met in Cluj during the summer of 1991, our growing friendship and trust became a gift beyond her own initial English rendering of *California (on the Someș)* for me to work on as co-translator. In fact, her explanations and advice to me, in our exchanged emails, almost wrote this introduction for me.

More than a few things I found in my notes and my emails from Ruxandra might be helpful to the reader. Or at least of interest. The first is kind of obvious, since it set the book going: the Eagles' song "Hotel California," from the mid-1970s, played a role that under the communist dictatorship had a more politically pointed ethos than it had in the West, rather than countercultural. At the time, this was, in fact, true of many facets of Western culture, for instance pop music, movies, TV, all of which were restricted under the Ceaușescu dictatorship. But for the poet herself, in a personal, sentimental sense, this effect was also what could be characterized as *Proustian,* like the evocative power of his famous *madeleine.*

For Ruxandra, the Eagles in particular also provided a kind of pretext for her belief in poetry as a supreme art, and more specifically the Doors, who are never mentioned or quoted in the poem: in the author's terms, "shamanistic" or "jimmorrisonian," with "underground music and image." And she added, there's "a pinkfloydian mood in my book (a psychedelic one, from time to time, when my memory is running water)." The fluidity of memory is a process that still continues, for her "California," she commented to me, "is running its waters until now." She has already added twenty pages more but has no plans either to stop (as her Author's Introduction remarks) — or to publish the New California.

As I knew, and Cesereanu observed, *California (on the Someș)* signifies a shift in her influences: "my poem is a flower-power one," as one of her messages described it, "a late flower-power in Romania and in a way, is a non-European poem…. It is I am sure my first book of poetry where my relative is not Europe and *les poètes maudits,* but American poetry and America…" The reader may notice a Ginsbergian formula (to me, also Whitmanesque) that repeats with some variation: "And then we knew." As translator, I varied the phrase more often than in the Romanian original. If this seems a sin, *mea culpa,* I fess up — I found it unduly stiff in its repetitions. To me, the small modifications are rather like adding the word "river," for instance, when the name Someș is mentioned, especially early in the poem, in order to situate the reader.

One last comment, about the structure and the pattern of fonts: it was quite apparent to me as I worked on the poem based on Ruxandra's English versions, and I knew it was something I had to ask about. So I wasn't surprised that she described the differences in the sections as huge. What is usually the opening section (plain Roman font) is "a real (or surreal) description" of the Someș riverside in the summer (one that, she added, "will become cosmic from some point"). The second part, in italics, constitutes what she termed "metapoetry, a meditation about poetry in time" and why she trusts it. And the third section (in bold italic) is usually concerned with memory running back to childhood and youth. However, Ruxandra went on to make clear to me, from the middle of the book to the end, these are "intentionally mixed." In fact a reader can see anomalies even earlier than that.

As the sections flow on and Ruxandra Cesereanu seeds *California (on the Someș)* with her conscious and subconscious revelations, like the shells she throws into the river, I hope as translator that readers will share what moved me, and more: its psychological power, imagistic clarity, surprise, complex emotions, poetic depth, and ritual grace.

California
(on the Someș)

Author's Introduction

In the spring of 2013, I bought a bicycle. I'd wanted a bicycle since I was a little girl, but for all sorts of reasons I'd never gotten one. My first bicycle rides along the bank of the Someș River were always with a hand on the brake, because I knew I risked hitting little kids, strollers and tricycles. In a short while I became used to taking out my bicycle every evening to ride on the rough, unweeded path near my apartment building, then in the Rose Park and finally along the asphalt road near the river as far as the Garibaldi Bridge in my home city of Cluj. I had become a habitué of the twilight and the Someș when something else took place. Coming home on my bicycle, I heard the low drone of guitars and isolated voices: a group of boys and girls strummed and sang the Eagles' song "Hotel California." The sound of the guitars and those teenage voices, some thin and high, others hoarse, made me slip back in time to when I was a teenager myself and sang to a guitar with my high school and later my university friends the very same song I heard now, improvised once upon a time with great frenzy, on the bank of the Someș, on the island called Dog Island or at the parties of graduates or students who thought themselves the center of the universe. From this moment of my going back in time, everything here began: it triggered an entire book made of a single long poem about childhood, adolescence, young womanhood and maturity. And about my faith in poetry.

So like the river swollen after a rain, my California on the Someș kept on growing. It hasn't reached its end and, in fact, never will.

On a dark desert highway, cool wind in my hair…

The avalanche started with boys and girls bewitching a guitar on the bank
        of the Someș River,
in this way memories and poetry began to cascade within me.
First, my eyes contracted into a single lens in my forehead,
a camera filming and dollying.

A lady of seventy or more stood in the river slapping her legs,
        her skirt rolled up,
as Hotel California enchanted the guitar's belly like a joint.
My bicycle became a musical instrument,
the Someș suddenly smelled of hippie days.
It was the summer of an explorer in the colonies
sporting a striped t-shirt and fisherman's bermudas.
Along the river, lawnmowers made waves in the grass
and dogs licked their masters' hands.

And then we knew:
we're the drug-addicts,
the ones who still believed in the huge shapes in the public square,
in the surfaces etched with hollows.

The sea shells from Paris, kidnapped long ago from Rue Monsieur le Prince,
the shells that I later threw into the Someș: look, they've grown fertile
and become the shells of vertebrates for reapers on the riverbed.
Once upon a time I stole them and gave them to the innocents,
who believed in me.
Inside these shells can be found all the childhood of the earth mixed with water.

*

Two men kept laughing as they rolled in the grass, their cell phones stuck
     to their bellies,
babies squealed in strollers, shrunken like mice dried out by the heat,
the city swelled with stench in its armpit,
the town was a cherry pie fallen on the asphalt.
The river rushed at the walls.

And we knew:
we are living the beginning and the end, backwards.
When carcasses disintegrate at the border of the sky,
we'll stuff their eye sockets with old newspapers.

The sea urchins pricked my soles in an Athenian bay
where teenagers leaping with shouts from the rocks
have scratched the name of an arrogant place known to them only: Sepolya City.
I took home cosmic sea-urchin carcasses,
and set one of them in the river water, even though it had crumbled.
But Sepolya City will never need to grow in the mists of the Someş.

*

On the riverbank, Saint Michael's church stepped down from its stilts,
kids with slingshots cracked the stained-glass windows.
The Insomnia Café stank of piss and unwashed poets,
in Club Zorki the pianos were smashed.
Inside the River Bar the diluted morning took on the sickly hue
       of hospital walls,
on the terraces around the Carolina Obelisk
the apocalypse of the new millennium had cast lots.
King Mathias himself went to the Someş to bathe.

I'm constructing this poem joist by joist.
I conceive it as a ziggurat.
Confused memories anoint my retina.
My eyes are now the origin of a poem writing itself.

In kindergarten we napped on cots folded from the wall,
dozens of little girls with bows in their hair.
I was the only one with cropped hair and dressed like a boy,
I wore a sweater and had tassels on my cap.
Afternoons, the matrons put us down to sleep
after we'd drunk tea laced with bromide.
Then the river journeyed across my back like a toy train.

*

Bits and pieces of people circulated in the suburbs,
bodies attenuated in wispy circles,
skins smelling of cotton clothes.
Beyond objects, the brain was insoluble,
a midget afloat on an abandoned dock.

Cigarette packs functioned as a social preservative.
The university building was covered by graffiti,
the letters' moisture healed the malady of writing.
Hotel California on the Someș kept wandering with tricycles and little kids.
Only gravediggers could be found in the abandoned houses.

And suddenly we understood:
our marsupia will shelter the creatures of the new ghetto,
so in this way we'll add to the family photos.
We're the sleepers in padded car parks.
There are no xeroxed miracles.
On the Someș, boys and girls sang till they got hoarse,
their teeth yellowed from cigarettes and peanuts.

The big shells I'd taken once upon a time on Long Island,
while two strangers told stories about the aurora borealis
and I, the third stranger, could not swim in the ocean.
The waves were walls.
I threw one of the shells in the Someș like a seed
and out of it the Empire State Building grew on the riverbank
*   like an electric pillar*
from which the world's poetry revealed itself as a pasture.
And so I returned to the beginning.

*

Liquid scenes.
Our happy swimmers' chests and the hydrated wigs in the ambulances.
On the Someş, sheets of tin wrapped around our cerebellum
before its execution by the afternoon's sleep.
The river watchmen had bottles of beer in their pockets,
stains on their hands from stretching a map of destruction.
House pets scratched their cages for air holes.

And we knew:
look, we're burning the refineries and blessing the sunflower.
Poetry is a bay of iodine!
The sunflower sticks itself under my eyelids.

The shells we found on the island where we cooked potatoes in ashes
as I hopped about in the undershirt of a child wanderer with burnt lips,
the shells I squeezed tight in my hands
as I floated on a rubber raft on the river alongside other paddling kids,
later I buried these shells at the mouth of the Someş,
hoping that someone would find them.

*

Intoxicated by Hotel California we kept making a racket,
awakening the neighbors hidden in their pantries.
Our uproar was epidermic.
We were carnivorous, our desolate eyes afflicted by knowledge.

It was the day of the dead when next I flew across the waters.
On this day of memorial candles I always recall
that I intended to be a nun.
I used to believe that a monastery was an apprenticeship in poetry,
and poetry a flesh and blood nun.
But many years have passed since then,
now I wear high heels and my ears are pierced.
On the day of the dead something in me turns purer,
like a door thrown down by arms gloved up to the elbow,
poetry like a monastery collapsed on its black-winged stilts,
and my former nun's habit hangs on a coatrack in the hall.
Do you know what happens when a bag is closed too tightly?
It doesn't split in only one place
but bursts everywhere it's closed.

"The holiday took a train to France, left lickety-split with ants in its pants.
come on, kids, play hooky from school, burn every book, break every rule,
hurry and smash the building to rubble, kill the teachers on the double,
pull down the streetlamps too, let's melt the city to goo" –
we'd screech like this, chirping like mid-June sparrows,
hidden whenever it rained inside our blanket-hut so long ago.

*

Near the river, human cells clumped together in a beehive,
the water an immaculate common grave
lined with lovers' tongues.
A kiss transformed into a beautiful crime,
the heart opened the lotus flower of the belly.
On the Someș floated garlands of dandelions,
men with orange belts shouted to an Indian god:
have we arrived at the Ganges? are we now in Shiva's narcosis?

The fever I live steals under the rocks,
but I hold it tight in my wrists, in my fists, in the core of summer.
Poetry is a railroad station with many waiting rooms.

Once upon a time, during the dog days, I ran through the enormous pipes
where workers were excavating trenches for sewers.
Then the sewers turned into human poetry-tunnels.
I traveled on the Budila-Express for a morning of the young ladies.
In a book of winter, staring at lighthouses, shop windows and photographs,
the electric snow lay below the flags.
In the end I found the final armor.

*

We're sweating, we're summer locusts.
Standing in the river we're poisoned
like Chinese officers around the ancient dead emperor.
Our ribs, filled with snowflakes,
hang loosely from abundant flesh.
There's so much summer that even a knife can't scrape it off.
Someone sticks little flags along the riverbank.

And then we knew:
we're conquerors who purify their intestines with fear,
victors with a delicate goiter.
We sing Hotel California
under the improvised shower of a washbowl and a bottle cut across its throat.

The yellow shells I patiently collected in the land of the minotaur
I tossed into the Someş for luck.
From these shells grew the erased photo of the arms trafficker
who was once the young poet I loved so much.
His faded clothes at maturity were my battle flag,
his aqueous eyes my power.

*

Our blood is tar with reddish irises,
corpuscles stirred into river water to reveal
the rot that loads our lives in sacks.
The hospitals have emptied the aquariums of bipeds,
nobody knows how to swim in mothers' wombs,
nobody has a diver's air hose.
The trams from the city center have arrived at the riverbank,
they hibernate for a while, then sing in a choir.
The cigarette-butt windows have disintegrated.
We're shore crabs of the springs, we grow syringes instead of claws.

I found Hotel California when I was teenager,
I was in blue jeans but had never heard of hippies,
those days my uniform was disco.
I had a college number sewn across the chest
of my school uniform, 356 or 453,
I was a city girl, though I played the guitar along the river
and puffed empty straws to ascend to Nirvana.

And then we figured it out:
poetry is hashish,
we'll devour birds of cocaine
and sleep in the bright lights.

*

The Someș river is a truck full of coffee,
a large box padded with raffia.
Here bicyclists look like snails without shells.
At the crossroads Hotel California can be heard,
guitars stick to the sternum –
little horses of wood.

We made up our minds:
we'd trick the lobotomy,
we'd wrap the minimalists in their gauze,
we'd live in maximum land, no adhesive across our mouths.

We sang on Dog Island when we skipped school at midday,
the river reached our hips and became a belt,
we rolled up the tunics of our school uniforms,
munching on breadsticks with little mouse teeth,
and imagined we were doing a striptease
for the watchers openmouthed on the shores.

*

The choir of watchmen: their words smelling of musty fur.

After a rain on the river, a postcard made of scraps:
corks, shredded bags, plastic sunglasses, unglued labels, slices of baguettes, a
cardboard gun, seeds, sliced strawberries, soggy chips, branches with cherries,
crushed cola bottles, badges, rubber medals, lipton teabags, schweppes,
        pigeon feathers.
The bloated bladder of the drunkards at the foot of the bridge,
a trumpet player bandaged in foil,
his arteries clogged by smoke and alcohol.

All these are dead weight.

One day in the center of the city I knocked on the door of a poet
who was not part of the usual pack.
We sat like two fish in twin aquariums,
then the glass broke and water invaded the lungs.
Near us was a trash bin full of flower stalks,
we were humble and ashamed to speak,
we held our hands in our laps like widows,
until it became possible for us to be marked on our foreheads
with a pale yellow spot so as to be recognized.

You were an expert in borders so I was able to talk about
the zone inside and another zone outside,
about how I kept to the limits.
Your voice came from far away,
so I felt that madness was something peaceful and fresh,
a delicate object in the breast pocket.
I sensed you were a shepherd of birds.
You sat beside me on a bench in the city not far from a trash bin.

Suddenly a camera flash captured us.
My small wisdom looked like a feather wafted over your head,
and we were put in the coffin of a postcard.

*

Myopic under the streetlights cockchafers dove at my eyebrows,
the mown grass shivered on the asphalt,
a boy threw a girl into the Someş after kissing her like a clown,
dogs mated rowdily under the broken benches.
This world was tactile behind the fences.
Our teeth no longer chattered in our mouths,
our hair no longer could fall,
and the alarm never rang morning or evening.
It was a summer of luxury.

A season of knowing:
we grew in the glare of the lights,
we buried infirmaries, confiscated their supplies of cotton-wool.
We made tapestries in our skulls with their electric network.

Once upon a time the train from the Balkans entered the water
        between the pillars,
when I saw the lagoon ripped out of the winter landscape,
I trembled, my mouth melted to molasses.
Then I yearned to transport Venice to the Someş,
along with its obsessions and microbes.
But details put their mark on the facts differently.
The Venetian boy, my first storyteller of Venice's waters,
I left there hostage to his numb ventricles.
The water of the lagoon remained just for him,
in a pocket with tangled plastic bags.

*

The city poem roasted in the Someș like buttered corn on the cob,
yellow grains launched a hepatitis of the eye,
the river's sputum mixed with spinal marrow.

And then we decided:
we wouldn't raise a banner, just memories to keep the heart in working order,
like a flag, uranium getting pumped through the blood.

When I was eighteen I climbed San Michele on Capri,
here I found the ruins of a malevolent emperor's villa.
Here I received a gift from on old priest,
a brown shell like a knee.
At home, I wanted to throw the shell in the Someș,
but I had a weakness for emperors.
For a long time after my wedding, I kept the shell hidden under the bed.

*

My body floated in water covered up my face,
but my eyes could see and never had enough of it.
An old man holding a child's hand leaned on a balustrade,
empty bottles snagged along the banks of the river.
A man waited there for a water sacrifice,
someone else emerged from a tent eating a ham sandwich.

And then I knew, submerged in the river as I was:
never shall we have scissors for pockets or sprinkle flesh with alcohol,
but we'll remain between our wads of psychic fleece,
euphoric like bear cubs with muzzles moistened by bees.

In the omphalos of the imperial city there's a fountain of desires
where bearded horses and men burst forth trumpeting from seashells.
Here I sat and laughed with another lioness,
imagining how to move this **Fontana** *of desires to the Someș.*
With a helicopter, just as the statue of Jesus
once upon a time was carried in a famous movie.
But this **Fontana** *did not permit us to keep her*
in the opening at our breast,
just to touch her like a cousin or an aunt.

*

This summer disfigures no one.
This summer isn't agrarian except superficially.
Hidden within it, passions, desolations and miracles.
This summer has no genitals.
Its wagon of dry lemons is pungent with its sharp smell.
Rusty razor blades, forgotten on a windowsill.

And then we knew, we saw it all:
hydrochloric acid on the artisans' hands,
holidays with nights like fast days,
hidden dementia in the cornfields along the railroad tracks,
the scent of oils and hot porno sex-toys.
We were precisely that, for an imploded summer.

I was sitting on a suitcase in the high school courtyard
before going to summer camp.
I was thirteen, fourteen, fifteen.
Dresses packed like paper napkins,
sandals like lovers,
transparent rouge with a strawberry scent
and a dizzy heart pounding out an awaking.
I was eager to fall in love with a boy in a rocker tee-shirt
who would tenderly whisper to me, "oh, baby!"
while we danced to the blues.
To gaze up at him as at a dealer in indulgences,
then transform summer into a genetic motel
where my girly cells would become a garden of waters.

*

The Someș is a hypodermic, its glass misted over from breath,
a door handle I'm pressing on to let the liquid behind the door spurt out.
The words of watchmen printed in e-newspapers.
The words of watchmen without their makeup.
Wrapped in cellophane: skin, numbers, home furniture,
covered and uncovered with figures of speech.
Only a city poem could break the laws and reveal itself
not even wearing a paper helmet on its head.

And so we knew:
poetry is underworld, poetry is the way out,
it is the spinal cord with clothespins on it
and the harpoon thrown deep in the thorax
where a derrick keeps pumping oil.
Poetry has no need for watchmen.

A scene along the river, a year ago:
in a rainy twilight I saw a man and a dog
with a bottle of rum in a bag overturned in the wet grass.
Meanwhile raindrops kept falling like a comb with missing teeth.
I was no longer thinking of friends' love-ulcers
but only of that dog and that man in the rain beside the bottle of rum.
The thing most alive was that half-empty bottle
overturned in the grass like a woman,
wrapped in the bag as in a ballerina's skirt.
Through the swollen tube of the bottle
desires could be seen as geometric formulas,
ideas that hadn't yet yielded to chloroform.
On the bottle, rain told a story
in which beings with a kind heart were absent.
The sage in this image was the dog,

his tail lying across the short-necked bottle of rum,
as if waiting to be blessed and to summon angels to the burial feast and to sing:
Hallelujah, oh Lord, send us rain until we have pickled the jugular,
until skin is blistered and breath is cooled.
We are a trinity of misery:
a man, a dog and a bottle of rum overturned in the grass
in a rainy twilight along the river.

*

Gypsy girls skipping in rubber boots through the Someș,
fishermen with hats and waders,
ducks from Finland dabbling here, there,
the smoked homeless dozing in the grass like bumblebees.
It smells of old sulfur,
day makes night putrefy,
noon is a ferocious clock with greased little wheels.
The lacquered toenails of teens in shorts,
their insolent buttocks.
It's a lustful summer.

These could be postcards from anywhere,
but summer's bunker gulps everything down
with its hippopotamus mouth.

We needed to know beyond knowing:
what remains after poetry when nobody knows what poetry is?
I find myself now under words, on a platform.
The summer poem, hanging from eyebolts, doesn't have to account for anything.

Sometimes, when I'd go to my grandparents' house in the north,
I'd find abandoned horseshoes
on the riverside where I'd laze about.
I always picked up a horseshoe, cleaned it in the water, then bit it gently
so I'd have good luck when I became a bride.
The river was sweet, the horseshoe salty,
and it seemed to have emerged out of a story from long ago.
The fish in the barrels at the grocer's
were steeped in clumps of salt.
In my grandparents' world, the Someș flowed softly.

*

A lonely man measures the river with a scarf
that was worn by the woman who abandoned him.
A boy who waits and waits for vacation to come
is now at the station with a relative pushing him
on to the train, ordering him not to do anything stupid.
With his unfinished voice, the boy keeps imitating the guitar
      from Hotel California.
A fourteen-year-old girl was supposed to blow his mind
with her Western dresses and scarves.
Several years later the boy will throw himself into the Someș,
the girl become a hooker in order to survive.

A pocket atlas: my Someș can be found in The Transylvanya.
This Transylvanya *is a poetry-drinking zone.*
*With a couple of letters more or less, we're building poetry factories
and changing the world.*

*Among the rocks of Moon Beach I didn't pick up even one shell
and I didn't sow in the Someș anything stolen from the pirates.
At this point in my poem, Greek memories are confused with Paris memories.
My zodiac twin knew death and barely escaped by the skin of her teeth.
I stayed with that beautiful woman on the Seine,
in one of the rocky nests of the Pont Neuf
or with our legs dangling down some stairs
as if we were acrobats on a rope.
I understood that someday she would become a shamaness,
so I'm setting her in my poem like a painted wooden doll.*

*

I am glorifying the iodine-tinted summer when ratcatchers chase after moles.
Along the riverbank are playground slides and nesting boxes for pigeons,
also church banners from bygone winters.
Dark red tennis courts await the roulette players.
At dawn Hotel California can be heard shrill like a train whistle.
A land of burnt sugar awaits us.

Then we were sure:
we're the losers of the keys,
the permanent tailors of words eviscerated from copybooks,
we're the epico-lyrical recidivists of a city of clay.
We're storytellers with jaws broken like ampoules.

For the myopic man with seventy invented names,
I never picked up a single shell.
Nor did I write anything for him.
But I was in his house and slept there.
I ate, and drank, and played with a Tarot deck,
there in the region of the Maritime Ode.

*

The glands of the river, sometimes swollen, sometimes atrophied.
Liquid solace overflows the riverbanks.
Peace within oneself, a lifetime persecution,
peace with others, a genetic anomaly.
But now the Someș covers everything
and throbs like Hotel California,
where even gorillas are happy.

So then we knew:
our scalps that the river baptized with wet dynamite
have renounced nihilism.
On the Ganges, ideology doesn't exist,
nor any dictionary of language's origin.
Red neon signs on the hills over the city
and a millennium of promises scented with camphor.
In the end, the arrogant breast of poets.

When I saw the Mississippi for the first time,
my adventures were not at all finished.
High water behind the levees cast a spell over a city turned topsy-turvy
by white nights, voodoo queens and former beatniks
still connect through their moustaches to a heresy.
And the heresy took the form of a submarine near the church in the central square.
The Mississippi spat out jazz garnished with grilled white alligator steak,
and we, skinned by poetry, were kept under hypnosis for the tongue of a
        new Jimi Hendrix.
My second time in New Orleans,
someone drew with a stick on wet sand
the outline of a kingdom which was still unknown among seers
but already had the structure of glory.

*

In the evening, the banks of the Someș echo with the barking of dogs
and the rustling of other creatures asleep between tree stumps.
But the watchmen chase away people in parrot-bright sweaters.
The watchmen allow only customary poetical things.

I'm from the Neolithic.
I fill myself with poetry.
I was just born for the third or fourth time,
but neither soldier nor priest.

During summer, once upon a time, I stayed with my girlhood friend,
smoking candy cigarettes on the riverbank, telling stories about people and things.
I still believed I could really die for her, if I had to.
And she'd do the same for me.
But then her mind became broken.
In this way, pathology was born.
Friendship along a river lasts only in poetry.

*

I want to reach the river's mouth.
I'm smoking Virginia Slims and watching summer from the balcony.
Kids are playing with rubber cushions,
swatting one another over the head and laughing without pity.
My fingers burnt from the nightlight, I touch my cup of tea, half empty.
The trams bulge with people like overripe pears.
Nobody is playing on the swings.
On the ground, a few paralyzed insects.

Within the brown vortex of the river there's a Himalayan peak,
but the Someș watchmen have cataracts.
The Himalayas are invisible from their watchtowers.

This is a videoclip.

Near the dock, black water lapping over the tips of our shoes,
once again we cast a spell on the Danube as it curves across a notebook.
First we revile the Danube, then we bless her.
Poetry and stories like a marketplace spring forth from the black water
or illuminations like peppercorns.
Things multiply or decrease because of the mouths gaping open at her chest.
It is a summer of strata, of departures.

*

The Someş is ink and a shop for black bread
when it rains without stopping, and everything heaps together until
      it all rusts.
Old ladies with a fancy hat disappear from the kiosks on the riverbanks,
old gentlemen with a pince-nez bury themselves in sand.
The sun burns on till the very end.
The river grows thick as halvah.
From the windows of apartment buildings,
housewives throw scraps to putrefy in in the water.
Men in undershirts guzzling beer fill the workshops along the river.
They no longer can tell if it's summer or winter.

I know why the city smells of bitumen as does poetry:
human misery remains a sort of pharmacy.
This city's poem is made of sailors' knots.

Nobody was dipping their legs in the Thames
when we climbed down near the reconstructed ship of Sir Francis Drake
to gather gray shells.
Passersby hurried after me, invading the water's muddy edge.
Later, at Henry the Eighth's pleasure palace,
we missed the boat back to London,
so we sat on the dock and kissed like a pair schoolmates
while fishermen threw shy glances from the opposite side.
Then we said together, from inside our kiss:
a human life has gone by with our love, hasn't it?
Later, looking at the bridges of the City at dusk,
you tenderly took my head in your arms like a visored cap.
We laughed and feasted for a last time,
immersed in the English waters.

*

Rains pierced through portholes,
rains stripped our singer's flesh.
On the riverside, puddles look like cow eyes,
we're jumping in the puddles, splattering mud on our chests.

The body felt as if it was coming apart,
legs dancing in Roman sandals,
thighs in garlands of moon flowers with milky sap.
The sulfur season reaches us only at night
when macerated stinks congregate in the watchmen's drowsiness.
The hawkers of roast pistachios shout across the water
to those washing linens in the Someş.
We're beside the Ganges but our country's in decline.
Where could the gods have gone, tumefied with jewelry?
We're weeping in their laps.

So then we saw the truth:
We shouldn't make deals with the bureaucrats of the afterlife.
Meanwhile the Sunday brass band floats down the river sitting
           on little prayer chairs,
we'll undress the angels and whisper obscenities to them.

At the tip of the island, surrounded by breakers,
the rain reached us as we stayed in the closed entryway of the little church.
And then you made a door of your body,
sheltering me with your long-sleeved shirt,
and you whispered joyfully:
God left us here alone together, beyond the world,
that we should be renewed.
The life between us is like a healthy son,
born after thirty years of marriage.

*

The riverbanks were terracotta.
In the grass, lost ping-pong balls.
My grandfathers' well from long ago had been moved,
and the bucket that every summer I stared into at my own image:
I wanted to be a superstar.
The Someș chewed tobacco like a tall goldsmith, belly hanging over his belt.

Green clings between the rocks.
Someone is slitting a hen's throat near the river,
Her head jumps at me and chases me far from the pack.
Summer is a basin for hundreds of apartments.

I finger the river on a kitchen apron and imagine I'm immersed in the Ganges.
Here I shall be baptized, here I shall give my death rattle.
In the last end, everything is liturgy or gruel.

The greenish water around the monastery
swirled near the hut where a cat had her kittens.
The small mews of the kittens kept us awake all night,
even the thieves on the hill fled to escape the crying.
In the morning, I jumped in the river in my shirt, angering the fishermen.
Nuns were cloistered within the smoke-covered walls.
I was twenty-seven years old and had an emerald ring in my ear.

*

The Someș has a ford like a font.
The sour moans of those singing Hotel California can still be heard.
Gums taste of calcium, dust strikes the cornea.
Masons go on scrubbing their overalls with earth in the river.
Everyone will want to submerge in the Someș as in a satchel.
On the banks, stinging nettles grow like forests.
In the ditch, feverish frogs scarcely breathe,
for kids steal them from beneath the rocks wanting to hang them.
At the far end of the riverbank, lovers caress.
Windmills heat up like electric stoves.
Drunks push one another down in the foliage along the river,
their pockets ripped by hands they don't know how to use.
Workers from the power plant smoke Turkish style,
their liver is a stuffed bird.

We see, hear, touch, smell a different world.
Even the tongue is a thigh.

When I arrived at the Jordan River, I became unleavened bread.
The devout wrapped themselves in bed sheets and immersed.
Plump fish and beavers both showed up
to eat breadcrumbs from the tourists' hands.
A heedless woman went swimming in her teensy-weensy bikini,
finally the souvenir vendors pulled her out of the holy waters.

*

Two brides in black tulle dresses along the Someș,
two women thin as twigs in the foreground of a photograph.
Above the river, a couple of legless men
chat together on their low, three-wheeled carts.
On the bank, in swim trunks, men flex their bricklayer's muscles,
      tanned tar-dark.
Teenage girls with pink caps whistle by on roller skates,
shifting their knees likes Chinese contortionists.
A blind teenager rides his bicycle,
his father caresses the handle bars with little whispers like a stalker.
It's a hot Bombay summer.

The first thing in the world:
my head born red as blood, like a wounded mouth.

A photo with the huge shell from Santorini.
The rugged object resembled me as a fetus.
Life was like a red onion.
The shell was an amorous object,
I pressed it to my breast as I napped.
I found myself in a funnel.

*

A flood of water was released over the dam
and the grass drowned,
the river seems a pale blue walrus.
The boundary between worlds becomes transparent.
A Japanese man who lives in the city saw the water as a trampoline.
He's glad to be inside the Zone
so he can glimpse the river's entrails.
The Someș is an immaculate conception.

Once upon a time an Anti-California could be found here.
Neurosis in sacks of cement and blues in cans of peas.
But now the blackness within me has escaped through my ribs.
My skeleton is pure.
I'm drawing poetry and writing Ichthys.
Ichthys *is poetry.*

I was coming along winding lanes and terraces that block the view
when suddenly Trani Cathedral stuck to my clavicle.
It was an albino pugilist.
I stood in the loggia of the cathedral, covered by a blazing sky.
Solitude was warm and natural there.

*

At the time when Anti-California could be found on the Someș,
people ingested drugs to forget the schism.
After internecine wars, California arrived at the river,
then shores were hung with tapestries and lullabies.
This was when I first started to believe a little in the peace of God.

The cold rain punished the earth like a feral cat.
On the riverbank, two bodies kept rubbing against each other.
Clothes were all but open, but love never emerged from there.
Just little wet moans on reddened skin.
Those bodies transformed into broken objects.
Then the squeaks of the two collapsed skins were heard faintly.
I felt my own carotid like a button on my dress.

First of all search for love in yourself, you told me.
Search for what poetry is, follow to the end.

*

My eye sees through a gummy retina.
On the riverside a kayak waits filled with cats in warm-up suits.

I was 18 years old when I swam to the wreck.
Boys pissed in order to mark their territory, but also out of fear,
then we all became deaf for several minutes,
as if in the waters the road to Damascus gaped open.

You told me I could be a shaman,
a dust storm would be my organ of perception.
The storm is a woman, you told me,
as the moon was the first man of every woman and every man.

Twice we set out for Navaggio,
the bay with the wreck buried long ago in sand like a fish skeleton.
We never reached it, although we'd waited fourteen years.
The captain shouted, poetry cannot be found in a hole in the sand,
it's impossible for poetry to be buried.
Then the ship stopped in a cave where you almost died swimming underwater
(a rock obstructed my view).
See, this is poetry, you told me, soaked to the ski, with slices of light on your lips.

*

A little white house on the shore, jerry-built from a shipping container
or an American-Indian tent, made of shirts and towels,
where cabbage butterflies rest between boards.

Whoever is alone, is she a match for the uproar or for the silence?
Which of her vertebrae will set words in the proper order
to resonate like a contrabass?

Here I am, breathing.

My regression among stone-plants,
mangled images in the watery abyss,
a transparent hammock I wound around myself.
I am Nemo scrubbing a submarine lost in the last war.
Fishes flying as in my **Arizona Dream.**
The eclipse of the sun wrapped in satin,
the skin uterine, even though it had the taste of sandpaper.

*

A red London telephone booth
on the Someș, like a museum in miniature.
Bushes of rapeseed and wild roses twined together.
A little girl, a ball in her hand, stops and asks me,
Were you born here, on the Someș?
Garbage cans like at a subway entrance,
distributed by a green van,
while the elderly draw a chalk circle.
Were you born here, on the Someș? the little girl asks again.
Mister Caterpillar, a mushroom-man sketched by graffitists under the bridge,
stares at my bicycle,
his lips of dry ketamine.

What is self-extinction for the good of poetry? Is poetry the salvation of mankind?
Does suicide exist only so that something will remain after you, (un)readable?

A cross made of aluminum cups.
Someone died on the Aegean shore.
The boulders seemed Siamese-twin dolphins.
The sunset moved me to remember soldiers, poets, friends,
jumbled in a heap and covered by sand.

*

The river has wagons.
I stopped at the way stations along the shore, displaying photos from
      all over the world.
You're laughing at my proletarian beret drawn down over one ear.
My blue-jeans are stiff with dried mud.
Near us is a high-voltage transmission tower, overrun with weeds,
where teenagers used to climb high above, to scare the cops.
We're watching fishermen in a competition, with boots up to their knees
      like divas.
Your hunting boots are like jars filled with fish heads.

Friendship is our belief in a little god, without name, without territories.
It is said that, after rain, human faces are the color of tangerines.

Outside it was raining hard with big drops,
along the Someș there's only one man's leg and one dog's.
Then I started to talk about friendship and shame.
Could friendship on the riverbank perhaps be as strong as faith?
Animal neurons near a guilty silence.

*

A California with barges built on battered pontoons,
but so alive in my memory,
the memory of all who want to remember.
Street lamps with dead insects, mini-carriages for tourists.

California is a body of water beneath a spreading sun.

On the split planks of the floating docks, a snow of linden flowers.
Under the pipes of the hut where the watchman lives – a floating tree, snagged.
A green bridge reaching toward the shore, toward people.
We sat there writing,
we were joyous coffins, dismembered,
oars struggle against metaphors, banished briefly from the city.
Lifebuoys lettered in white mostly worn away over many summers
reeked of plasticized fish.
A little flag, lacking glory, at the mouth of the estuary
where thick ropes sleep in wooden chests.

*

Old men in a rousing drinking song.
We huddled by the campfire made from sawdust.
The sun *deep purple,* trombone, drum, accordion,
the season's high water on the river recorded amid clouds of mosquitoes.
Love and friendship,
a glass bridge impregnated by hoofs
and a vial of folliculin at maturity, broken on the wharf.
Life in transit.

And then we knew: the marine style of summer is innate.
Tin Jesuses stand at the crossroads in the little garden with poppies.

A swing could be found on the river along with other playthings.
We stayed at opposite ends,
bone on one side, skin on the other side, each with a small mound.
Poetry was explained as the quantum balance,
a tie game of bodies and sounds.
Then with the pair of little fiends, we arrived at the Sarmatian Sea,
we prayed and sang the Axion, after descending into secluded hermitages.
A dead woman in a cherry-wood coffin sang along with us.
On the Someș, old clothes, multi-colored, hung from the branches and
        draped the stones.
Grass had grown through the rails.

*

I open the gates just enough to enter the little darkness at
      the parched mouth.
Here it's the season of long summers, roosters can still be heard
      across the river.

And then I understand why I loved Odysseus and why I plucked out his orbs:
I needed to see through his eye sockets,
to invent a Saint Eulalia of poetry at any time.
Instead I chose Odysseus.
On a bench along the shore, an obese florist with hair dyed straw-color
orating in a drawn-out, orotund voice: we are in the naval sector of poetry.

That evening led to wild gestures during the dance.
There gathered behind my eyes our many adventures from our youth:
high above, in the amusement park, trying the pneumatic boats until faintness,
tracing Salvador's steps in the transparent cabin on the Costa Brava.
I kept writing all this. Murmuring Bar-ce-lo-na.
A seagull dove over my head thinking I was a plastic bag filled with dough,
fish as long as my forearms pushed plastic bottles out of the water
      with their snouts.
People took snapshots on the shore like at a fair,
where my layered skirt was an old movie, projected slowly,
my navy tee-shirt (do you remember?) was intentionally cut out on the chest.
A boy with mafia glasses and a retro hat kept playing a saxophone,
Barcelona was webbed by funiculars,
a metropolis of brazen, greedy birds.

*

On the shore, watchmen were living in huts of scrap metal,
sleeping on mattresses filled with corn cockle.
Out of orneriness they ate only pumpkin seeds and hooked shut
the trapdoor to the cellar from where the sour smell of pickles seeped out.
They were cyclopes.

And then you arose, Invictus, *from poetry's golden grotto.*
You, who stayed in a Provençal cage with the gang of analphabets,
you, who survived in an asylum, even you were a patriarch,
you, who have been an alcoholic, a suicide from car exhaust,
you, who lived a quarter of century when you were massacred
by invisible ink spattering from a computer.
Here, look at me, I'm making a vow, shaking my head, rocking my shoulders.

I found myself in a Smoky Zone
where poetry emerged gleaming like mist on windows.
Our boarding passes had been approved by scribes.
There I saw you for the first time, Invictus,
voyager returned from 83 to 25 years old,
fermenting poetry for rebels.
You had a blue-denim tunic
that the pilots had brought you from far away.

So I promised:
we'll never cower or be seduced, but we'll always be different, that is, **invicts,**
with mobile phones that penetrate the kingdom of heaven.

In the glass house with a pale green wool rug,
strata of words ripen that the watchmen will never reach.
Reality is a little Japanese girl kneeling in the airport,
eating chips and sucking on a baby bottle of mint tea.

Invictus, *great-grandfather, great-grandson,*
you alone sleep among flamingos.
Your lips blow bubbles of maraschino,
your nails have the strangest lacquers.

On the white sand of Ipanema
surfers rested with their surfboard under their heads.
The sea of Brazil was a septuple water.
At our back the two mountain-masters of the landscape,
Sugarloaf and Corcovado.
Jesus, thirty meters higher with a bracelet of clouds at his ankles.
I covered myself from head to toe in a scarf of melted linen,
and dug myself into a hollow in the sand.
Then you said to me, drink from this half-green coconut:
this is why once upon a time gods were born here.

*

Crow-silk over the swirling waters.
On the river, the fumes from car exhausts didn't reach us,
here human beings can feast in the water,
they are born anew with phosphorescent marrow.
Pensioners in pajamas come to the beach with blankets full of holes
and fall asleep in the grass as in a peapod.
Sometimes they smell of excrement, sometimes like a freshly bathed baby.

The Someș has lips parted on its forehead.
Along the edges, its temples are made of cigarette butts.
For a long time nobody has drowned in the river,
so no memorial offering of boiled wheat is floating on it.
The brown water is a harsh brandy with ravines.

The ziggurat has eyes, eyebrows and lashes worked in kaolin,
through complete vision annihilating the boundaries between cold people,
all upside-down on the Someș in buckets holding gifts.

The water of the estuary was broad like an ocean of hothouses.
I traveled half a day among docks and refrigerated warehouses
on a bus from the middle of the twentieth century.
The customhouse of the harbor was in a foreign church.
A gigantic fish that could feed a family of dwarfs lay belly-up on the shore
and a drowned rat, fat as a gander.
Here could be found the epigonic Cloaca.
Then you said: maybe we've arrived at the world's end
and the end of everything is right now.
I wore a violet skirt, I lay propped on your left hip,
stretching myself out behind the fishermen's backs.

Cortázar once wrote that Paris is a Buenos Aires.
I now write that Buenos Aires is a New York.
But who will remember the poisoned waters?

*

In such bright sun, shoulders are burnt beet-red.
On the river a ring of horses ridden by kids floats by,
and corrugated-paper ships.
It was like this in the times of the violet-blue river,
when dancing sailors were in the thumb-tacked posters
and thistles that covered the shores.
Thick black oil floated behind the serpentine.
But now, at midday, I can see something else, with the single eye
      in my forehead:
flattened dung on the asphalt near the dwarf maples,
planks with slimy snails and crows that are smoking.
On the shore, a woman with bare breasts sits reading a book.

I am writing about California on the Someş
and I can't stop because of summer.
I took out a wig.
I built a floating mailbox,
while jam was boiling in the pan.

When I was five I thought summer is a festival in India.
My dolls were made of mantras and incantations.

*

There was a bar brawl at the gates to the river, near the bridges.
The boatmen hadn't hands but prostheses, the wood faded from
       the dazzling afternoons.
Their chests were filled with strands of corn silk.

I wrote the history of unknown customs.
I inscribed it in calligraphy for strangers.

From the Monk's House and its gardens we took the path to the river
and arrived at the bank where Lady Woolf tied a boulder on her neck.
Beyond the hillocks of the meadow,
the locals advised us not to cross farther.
Then you banished the neurosis and told me breathlessly:
why search in anger for a stretch of river hallowed by a death long ago?
We're two living women, with men equally alive.
And then we took the road back to the city, whistling away the loss.
In a small river there's no reason to lose yourself.
Only in a whirlpool is it worth doing.

*

A forgotten memory, born from muddy waters.

Flashes are ping-pong balls that roll
to the feet of those who leap over them.
A memory about mr.-poet-with-cats is my ball now,
because when I was twenty I wrote him a letter
asking about the ship of fools.
He wasn't a master of rivers or waters, he kept a bevy of animals in his house,
and I recognized almost nothing of his pale melancholy.
I imagined him with Einstein's translucent mane,
hidden in a sleepy railroad station
while violinists in a snowy field played at four in the morning.
Sometimes I caught a glimpse of him staying at an inn with the ghosts
          of fellow writers,
a prisoner of a literary war.
Meanwhile I was in a delirium about the history of hanging witches.
Then mr.-poet-with-cats appeared, a street lamp in his hand,
and fallen down like a bell whispered,
explaining always the same thing,
exactly how solitude feels
and how nobody can burn it away, not even with a hundred candles.
Poetry is a spoiled object, poetry is the condition of human beings on a path
          to the ascetic.
For many years I kept his two-page letter about the ship of fools,
then I lost it or gave it to someone, I can't remember.
In the third millennium, old mr.-poet-with-cats had frost in his eye sockets,
but even so, nobody could confuse him with the fabled blind man
because his two companions entertained him day and night,
one of them clutching in his hand a crystal quartz that lit up the road,
the other mute, drifted over by snowfall.
A lifetime has passed since I saw mr.-poet-with-cats

with his telescopic eyeglasses and bohemian trench coat.
Now it's simultaneously morning and dark night with sea anemones.
I can remember the frost in his eye sockets, and I'm writing
on the label of a food can from the time of communism.
And while I write, I occupy myself gracefully as in a **lied,**
spelling out with exactness,
"if death no longer existed…"

The summer poem is a ship of fools marooned on the shore.
I'm both captain and sailor who writes in clay.
The tablets with writing are placed in storage and preserved for many years.

*

Our love is a little box
nobody is allowed to open and enter.

From California always another California gets born,
with warehouses and ferry boats day and night.
If memory is to finish its weaving,
then it must complete its shroud with embroidery.
But this work won't happen till after death,
when the band sets up the wind instruments in a lime pit.

Ten days before school was to start,
all of us pilgrims gathered to pop tar bubbles in the asphalt.
It was dark and our mingled voices told stories with extraterrestrials.
We'd spent the summer with grandpas, uncles, aunts and cousins,
our hair was cropped short, later it would reach past our shoulders,
we'd swum in the sea, climbed the mountains,
twittered like tom titmice in a tree
and thumbed our way to California.
Already it was the beginning of fall
and nobody had awakened from sleep with tongue plucked out.
We confessed to one to another like dwarfs,
we believed in summer holidays like a gospel,
a little gospel we learned by heart.
Here and now it's supreme Summer,
God came and never left.
God is not dead.

*

Sulfur, mud, damp, rankness.
Center of worlds of pestilence.
Usury, the mouths of sewers.
Magma and miasma.
The seaports and ocean cities
where dying is always in delirium.

Summer rhizome.
Poetry is born also from combustible substances.

After the expedition to the monasteries, where we traveled in a packed train
with a group of believers, faithful peasants hurrying to the parish feast.
We were penniless, with only a loaf of bread in a plastic bag.
This was why we sang all night long
for the celebrants who spent the night outside the monastery.
Later the guitarist and I awakened with a bottle of wine in his knapsack.
In the second-class waiting room,
girls in jeans poured the wine down their throats like ambrosia.
They swam in the Someș before midnight,
dressed just as they were.
The vacation ended but we managed first
to crochet wings out of cut newspaper,
even though summer had the smell of dried fish.

*

Tall weeds tangled along the walls of the river-buildings.
It smells like a wedding.
California is dressed in rubber, like a deep-sea diver.
Ravens drop stolen foil on the balconies.

Poetry became my sole possession.
Merchandise carried in a wooden soldier's suitcase
with a lock to be broken in case of need.

That afternoon I slept with the bible open in the middle, under my hips,
staying on the book as on a sheet stained by sanctity,
that afternoon as I proclaimed like a prophetess
that my little castle will be in a California on the Someș just in Ellada.
In that house of figs and pomegranates, I'll live with poetry as my crown.
I once closed the wound and varnished the cartilage
of a teenager who from the head of an island
had been tossing bottles with letters stuffed inside into the water.
He never knew that I buried him in poetry
and made his life a chapter in verses.

*

On Sunday, the Someș is perfumed with love,
and love is a telegram copied from books with queens and heroes.
Fishermen, in anoraks and with gypsy moustaches,
smoke Havana cigars and shout at the lovers glued to the high grass:
may you be saviors of the World!

Once we were romping around the fire like badgers,
goodbye dear summer, holiday goodbye, look! we're flying,
grannies kept crossing themselves at us naughty little devils,
it was high summer, the holiday was baking like a potato,
its core was roasting, but we kids cooled it with rock salt.

Suddenly we knew: we had arrived at the cavern of Black Jesus.
Poetry is a geyser in the middle of the cavern.

*

The rain spun around like a body in a shell.
Love is now in my room.
In this house, silence and night.
Morning arrives jamming feet into shoes.

The chapel on the rock was near the abandoned dormitories.
You opened the chapel, it was clean inside, and you said to me:
you can pray here every Sunday.
Meanwhile pieces of glass churned in the waves.
We began to search for sounds from our adolescence
that we hadn't shared, even though we had the same song-walls.
Smoke on the water + C'est la vie + Can't take my eyes off you
+ I will survive + By the rivers of Babylon + Dancing Queen.
And even before all these, fragments of spaghetti westerns.

Maybe memory is itself a scrap of California?

Darla dirladada je ne sais pas pourquoi vive la rose et le lila
caramels bonbons et chocolat je t'aime moi non plus.
Inside the chapel were ancient oil and crumbs of incense,
stained slips of paper, kitsch icons and a hole in the wall for breathing.
We lingered like an old fiancé, filtering prayer through our teeth.
June bugs landed on the dancers' dresses,
women had necklaces around both ankles.

Partirà la nave partirà dove arriverà questo non si sa.

*

At night tram tracks could be seen on the surface of the Someș,
while plastic bottles, half sunk in the river,
crackled like irreal buoys.
Several days after the drunkard's image of the tram,
you walked through the mist on a mirror of water
spread before a building with chandeliers.
Your black raincoat was an hermit's cloak at the world farthest end.
You can see, I told you, how the fog on the river made us remember ghosts.
Your eyes were bright like a little boy's and you prophesied,
Now nothing can frighten us, love is all-embracing,
annihilation has been eliminated for the time we have yet to live.

The power to write can be like any other power,
if there were no atrocity and pathos in its wake.

Then we tumbled back with the years
when on the bank of another river we took a one-night's cruise,
dancing on deck till our soles turned black.
We embodied sinuousness like bewitched cobras.
After the drink on the ship ran out
and what was left of the roast had been thrown overboard into the water,
we arrived at an island encircled by silvery reeds
where silhouettes of mist shivered in the sand.
Night dwellers showered confetti after us from bridges
and threw us kisses of farewell.
We returned home at dawn in a city devoid of breath,
convinced that death looks like a cruise with music, meat and booze.
Life is exactly like death,
and your hermit's seclusion could be the signature of this.

*

Nostalgia of the sterilizer.
I write and reminisce on the river, living many lives simultaneously.

And then I knew: the single eye in my head was an eel.
The eye was a wet mandible.

From the shore of Vama Veche to Lefkos village, we walked across the chitin
of crushed insect bodies to reach the sea in a cove under the headland.
Sometimes we both stood on boulders in the sheep cemetery,
touching the worlds gathered in a lighthouse on a desert island.
The old shopkeepers from the minimarket were soaking
in chemises hiked up to their knees, murmuring with pleasure,
the heat became refreshing like ice cream on a stick.
A sailor was whistling for the goats like a thief,
then chased them from the beach.

Love, like poetry, is a leprosarium joyously on strike.

Then our waiting cast lots.
In Eleusis I fell sleep in Pluto's cave,
my hat with a scarf tied about it like a chastity belt.
This hell was beautiful, this hell had sweetness,
the knowledge of hell was pure poetry.
Kore was happy in the house of Hades, with her verdigrised god.

*

Beneath the river were cities rich with water-tales.
That's where grandparents' old books are to be found.
Kids gathered under the bridge, glanced here and there through
      a royal charter,
drawing, cutting or adding words.

*Water is a mightier emperor than fire, because water always extinguishes fire.
Whosoever packs wells full of wood, to stop them up, knows that the purest water
originates from the realm where no human foot has ever trod. Both eyes get
plucked out from the thirsty bride, for water. God was born from rivers, and
likewise the Devil was born from rivers. God dispatched the Devil to bring Him
some sand, but the Devil concealed a few grains of sand beneath his tongue, that
he might have something that belonged just to him. When aided by the rivers, God
washed away the last grain of sand, He proceeded forcibly to cleanse the Devil's
tongue as well. The Earth is a sleeping fish: if it awakens, it begins to slip away. If
it weren't for the cock and the fish, Jesus would never have been raised from the
dead. When ancient witches die, it rains for seven days and seven nights, and the
river becomes a mountain of streams. The witches stand like trees upon the water
and never sink. When the Devil believes that the river flows with brandy, he
drinks until he collapses under the table. If you are dreaming, a fish means a
woman. On New Year's Eve, the waters turn to wine and the saints astride the
tuns float upon the river, like kings and lovers. Because of drunkards, God stole all
the wine but left a few drops for Mass. When little girls bury their dolls, it rains
until the river swells over its banks.*

And in the end the kids under the bridge have composed a new book
      with drawings,
from which not a letter has been cut.

*At the city gate, Dolorosa slumbers in the rain.
Nobody can hear whether she's quiet or weeping.*

In her arms she cradles a doll, and she sees only empty churches around her.
On the gray body of the Someș, a drowned man dreams.
Blunted river, you split the city like a living axe and you bleat licentiousness.

Cities with water-tales stay rolled in a ball at first, then unfurl.
I catch hold of the towns' hips when I dance in chiaroscuro.

*

The watchmen have started to rake the river
to remove larger stones and leave just pebbles.
They want to clean the river
so the Someș will be simple and clear.
They have decreed a quarantine,
they intend to split the muddy shores and turn them inside-out like long johns.
The island in the middle, with its pack of rabid dogs, they want to raze
        from the face of the earth,
then wrap it in sheets of cellophane, its back broken.
In the watchmen's huts, hospital attendants soon show up with scythes
        and mattocks,
arriving in a van with a tank of disinfectant.
It's not for nothing that they wear caps.
Their main instrument for extermination of rats is pincers several meters long.
All must be simple and clear, a river without fish,
without wild animals, just swill in a carafe.

And then you arose, Invictus, *man and dragon,*
with the whirlpool of ivy in the midst of the roiling waters,
a holy lining of poetry by theft.

Only the pilots knew you were subaquatic.
With your dragon's mouth, you shout to the watchmen: you are cyclopes!
Then you curse them, you cut robes of crow-silk and scarves of lianas.
Into their thorax, you stuff a turban of hair
so they can no longer comb it.
The watchmen turn mute, their teeth hook in the beaters' nets with their
        cruel maxillae.
Then life starts up anew, as in the beginning,
before there came cyclopes to the Someș.

From the maternity hospital, I was brought home to a rented house by the side
of the river.
All three of us, mother-father-and-me, lived in one shabby little room.
Swaddled in layers of linens, I screeched all the time at the top of my lungs.
One day, my parents both fled to the Someş
to escape the squeals of their newborn girl.
After several hours of solitude I learned what poetry is.
It was my first lesson.

*

The expansive episcopacy of the river
was always like a watershed.
After the Someș was left with its freedom of choice,
the river became a mythological object.
Behold: the lighted windows, the purple towers of the city of Cluj with
      the cross on Belvedere,
the evenings with sooty iridescence in the cheekbones, stuck in the channels,
the floating beds from the time of drought long ago
when the washerwomen sang until their mouths were in pain.
Horsemen dragged behind them, through the water, undergarments from
      the clotheslines
and called out skillfully pressing their short whips with their thumb.

The high-voltage towers turned into Eiffel Towers.
On the cables were cold paralyzed birds,
the river took on the color of blue oil.
Stones begun to grow like wisdom teeth.

When I was seven years old, I'd go fishing with my parents on the Someș
or on the nearby lakes.
Father sat on a little aluminum chair like a dwarf,
mother fished a little ways off, sitting on a stump.
Their silence was an unreal marriage.
I didn't understand at that time what poetry was,
but it seemed to be like the miraculous fishing narrated by the apostles of Jesus.
You never know if you'll have good luck and whom you'll be with,
or if you're a fisher of men.

*

My bicycle reached the streetlights near the little bat furs.
In the park's ring was a roller-skating competition,
the prizes, wooden toys and Rubik's cubes.
The master of the river pavilion along the river was Red Bull.

I'd known in secret that alphabets had detached themselves from the history
     of poetry.
It was said that poetry fulfilled spatiotemporal extinction.

I was caught in the waters
when the first walls collapsed and in their stead other walls arose.
The voices in my head spoke to me one after another, intermingling:
despite everything else you believe in salvation through poetry,
but we wonder if in truth you're saving only yourself or the others too?
An old poet I sometimes exchanged the letters from alphabets with
murmured to me between her teeth:
the ambulance doesn't always come,
for salvation is a travesty.

*

How many human lives were consumed in a single poem:
I fought on in the battle for poetry, I was resurrected,
and I made from memory a small pouch of incense.

I was all the river objects and the stones on the banks.
I heard music underground and beneath the heavens.
I colonized poetry.
My waters weren't typhoons and brought about no human death, but
      something else.

When I was born, I was laid in a little box of God, tied tight with a cord.
My mother had earrings like an African woman's,
my father cut the ribbon and I made my entrance into poetry.
My stillness then had previously been sound and fury,
tied with rope in a soldier's parcel.
The body and the lips became body and lips
only after the sound softened them and they took on a sheen.
I know that those never bound with rope live on somewhere,
those who have magnets in their mouth and bones of wool cloth.
In my little box from once upon a time, I stay and watch the world from far away,
then I tie my hair forever with the shiny rope,
so it won't fall over my shoulders like dark rain.
Because I have already made my entrance into poetry.

*

Under the ficus we sang, summoning shamans from the Someş.
The people beneath the hills came forth as though under a charm.
The cactuses on the apartment building's balconies
bloomed with tiny flowers like glass pearls.
Summer rippled with waves of grass under the heavens.
The land of puddles was ruined.

Some dance to remember,
Some dance to forget.

We started to swell with a vast water,
to know first of all the limits, then the core.
The Someş River metamorphosed into a mummified Indian head.
The waters were stirred up by sea-foxes,
striped dolphins dove with their long necks,
Jonah's whale became a spy.
Leviathan and the undines bet their breath at craps,
ocean-swallows soared through the waves, among barracudas.
Noah and Charon wash crumbs off their thighs, near lantern-sharks.
I kept shouting from the boulders, a megaphone pressed to my lips:
monsssterrr from Looochhh Nesss, rise from your depths and swallow me!
Eels and rays wrapped about each other like scarves.
But the last in the waters was the moon-fish that dwelled in the depths.
From his belly memories slipped away,
from out of his mouth issued forth words that did NOT exist
       in the beginning,
those words had been replaced.

And then we knew:
because of poetry our skin cracks open,

in our mouths we hide immortelles from the ancient kings,
and a little whistle hung around our necks summons darksome tigers.

We are the summer mediums,
musical instruments of ripening.
We wear glass-pearl masks but we are predators.

The beast and the king are inside us.
Behold, the time of outside has come, time beyond laws.

*

We are near the glowing cylinders on the Someş,
we have reached our destination,
transcended mortality.

Summer has become meta-time,
its heat is our cinema of mannequins,
their rind has been singed off.

The heart is the only law and the only dictionary.
All the other organs have been devoured,
and from the heart a new language gets born.

In this way we pierced the world's breast
and reached the raw fragment of the heart.
Invicti, *we enter the Acropolis now,*
where no distinction separates humans, animals, gods.

Poetry is alone, only poetry.

WELCOME TO HOTEL CALIFORNIA

Ruxandra Cesereanu has been acclaimed as one of the most important and prolific Romanian literary figures of today. She is particularly recognized for her achievements as a poet and novelist, especially the lyrical evocations of femininity and eroticism. She began her literary career as a new expressionist poet, then grew under the influence of surrealism and the Romanian movement that developed out of it, termed onirism, which Cesereanu thought of as becoming more of a dreamlike or psychedelic experience, in the term she coined a style *delirionism.*

Cesereanu's literary achievements include ten books of poetry: *Garden of Delights (Grădina deliciilor,* 1993); *Live Zone (Zona vie,* also 1993); *Fall Over the City (Cădere deasupra orașului,* 1994 — awarded the Poetry Prize of the Writers Association in Cluj); *Schizoidian Ocean (Oceanul Schizoidian,* 1998, 2nd ed., 2006); *The Crusader-Woman (Femeia-cruciat,* 1999); *Venice with Violet Veins. Letters of a Courtesan (Veneția cu vene violete. Scrisorile unei curtezane,* 2002, 2nd ed., 2016); *Kore-Persephone (Kore-Persefona,* 2004 — Prize for Poetry of the Writers Association in Cluj); *Coma* (2008 — Prize for Poetry of the Writers Association in Cluj); *California (on the Someș) (California (pe Someș),* including in a bibliophile edition, 2014); *Letter to a friend and back to the country (Scrisoare către un prieten și înapoi către țară,* 2018, 2019); and *Sophia Romania (Sophia România,* 2021).

Her work in prose includes the novel *Tricephalos* (2002, 2nd & 3rd eds., 2010, 2019), a book of short stories *Nebulon* (2005), *The Birth of Liquid Desires (Nașterea dorințelor lichide,* 2002), and the novel, *One Sky Above Them (Un singur cer deasupra lor,* 2013, 2nd ed., 2015).

Ruxandra Cesereanu also collaborated in a pair of experimental co-authored books: *The Forgiven Submarine,* written with Andrei Codrescu via an intense process of email exchanges (*Submarinul iertat,* 2007, and translated into English by Codrescu — published by Black Widow Press in 2009); and *The Otherland (Ținutul Celălalt,* written with Marius Conkan, 2011).

Three books of Cesereanu's poetry have previously appeared in English: *Schizoid Ocean* (translated by Claudia Litvinchievici, 1997); *Lunacies* (translated by Adam J. Sorkin, Claudia Litvinchievici and the poet, 2004); and *Crusader-Woman* (translated by Adam J. Sorkin, Claudia Litvinchievici, Madalina Mudure and the poet, and published by Black Widow Press, 2008). A book of her prose fiction, *Angelus,* was published in English in 2010, translated by Alistair Ian Blyth, and other books have been translated into French, Italian, Bulgarian, and Hungarian.

Cesereanu has also written analytical works breaking ground in the study of the Romanian *gulag,* political torture in the 20th century, and "the violent imaginary" in the Romanian mentality.

She was born in Cluj, Romania, in 1963, where she studied at the Babeş-Bolyai University, and now serves as a Professor at the Faculty of Letters (Department of Comparative Literature), a member of the staff of the Center for Imagination Studies (*Phantasma*), and director of the Creative Writing Workshops on poetry, prose and movie scripts. After earning a PhD in 1997 with a thesis about the Romanian detention memoirs and literature about communist prisons and camps, Cesereanu was the recipient of a Fulbright Grant to the US, affiliating with the Columbia University Harriman Institute in New York City (1999–2000).

Adam J. Sorkin, recently described by *Asymptote Journal* as a "star translator," has published more than sixty-five books of contemporary Romanian literature in English. Recently, in 2020, his books included *Cousin Shakespeare: A Tragedy in Five Acts* by Marin Sorescu, translated with Lidia Vianu (Caracal, Romania: Editura Hoffman), and three poetry collections: *A Spider's History of Love* by Mircea Cărtărescu, translated with seven co-translators (New York: New Meridian Arts), *Lavinia and Her Daughters* by Ioana Ieronim, translated with the author (Somerville, MA: Červená Barva Press), and *The God's Orbit* by Aura Christi, translated with Petru Iamandi (Wivenhoe, Colchester, Essex [UK]: Mica Press). In 2021, Sorkin published *Quarantine Songs* by Carmen Firan and Adrian Sângeorzan, translated with Alexandra Carides (New York: New Meridian Arts) and *Night with a Pocketful of Stones* by Traian T. Coșovei, translated mostly with Andreea Iulia Scridon (Talgarreg, Wales [UK]: Broken Sleep Books).

Sorkin's versions of a selection of Emilian Galaicu-Păun's poems, translated with Diana Manole, were honored with second prize in the 2017–18 John Dryden Translation Competition [UK], and his translation with Lidia Vianu of Marin Sorescu's last book, *The Bridge,* won The Poetry Society [UK] Popescu Prize for European Poetry Translation in 2005. Sorkin's other awards include the Kenneth Rexroth, Ioan Flora, and the Poesis translation prizes. For his translation activities he has been granted Fulbright, Rockefeller Foundation, Arts Council of England, New York State Arts Council, Academy of American Poets, Soros Foundation, Romanian Cultural Institute, and NEA support.

Adam J. Sorkin is Distinguished Professor of English Emeritus, Penn State Brandywine.

BLACK WIDOW PRESS :: POETRY IN TRANSLATION

BLACK WIDOW PRESS :: MODERN POETRY SERIES

RALPH ADAMO
All the Good Hiding Places: Poems

WILLIS BARNSTONE
ABC of Translation
African Bestiary (forthcoming)

DAVE BRINKS
The Caveat Onus
The Secret Brain: Selected Poems 1995–2012

RUXANDRA CESEREANU
California (on the Someş). Translated by Adam J. Sorkin
and Ruxandra Cesereanu.
Crusader-Woman. Translated by Adam J. Sorkin.
Introduction by Andrei Codrescu.
Forgiven Submarine by Ruxandra Cesereanu
and Andrei Codrescu.

ANDREI CODRESCU
Forgiven Submarine by Ruxandra Cesereanu
and Andrei Codrescu.
Too Late for Nightmares: Poems

CLAYTON ESHLEMAN
An Alchemist with One Eye on Fire
Anticline
Archaic Design
Clayton Eshleman/The Essential Poetry: 1960–2015
Grindstone of Rapport: A Clayton Eshleman Reader
Penetralia
Pollen Aria
The Price of Experience
Endure: Poems by Bei Dao. Translated by Clayton
Eshleman and Lucas Klein.
Curdled Skulls: Poems of Bernard Bador.
Translated by Bernard Bador with Clayton Eshleman.

PIERRE JORIS
Barzakh (Poems 2000–2012)
Exile Is My Trade: A Habib Tengour Reader

MARILYN KALLET
Even When We Sleep
How Our Bodies Learned
Packing Light: New and Selected Poems
The Love That Moves Me
Disenchanted City (La ville désenchantée)
by Chantal Bizzini. Translated by J. Bradford
Anderson, Darren Jackson, and Marilyn Kallet.

ROBERT KELLY
Fire Exit
The Hexagon

STEPHEN KESSLER
Garage Elegies
Last Call

BILL LAVENDER
Memory Wing

HELLER LEVINSON
from stone this running
LinguaQuake
Lure
Lurk
jus' sayn'
Seep
Tenebraed
Un-
Wrack Lariat

JOHN OLSON
Backscatter: New and Selected Poems
Dada Budapest
Larynx Galaxy
Weave of the Dream King

NIYI OSUNDARE
City Without People: The Katrina Poems
Green: Sighs of Our Ailing Planet: Poems

MEBANE ROBERTSON
An American Unconscious
Signal from Draco: New and Selected Poems

JEROME ROTHENBERG
Concealments and Caprichos
Eye of Witness: A Jerome Rothenberg Reader.
Edited with commentaries by Heriberto
Yepez & Jerome Rothenberg.
The President of Desolation & Other Poems

AMINA SAÏD
The Present Tense of the World: Poems 2000–2009.
Translated with an introduction by Marilyn Hacker.

JULIAN SEMILIAN
Osiris with a trombone across the seam of insubstance

ANIS SHIVANI
Soraya (Sonnets)

JERRY W. WARD, JR.
Fractal Song

BLACK WIDOW PRESS :: ANTHOLOGIES / BIOGRAPHIES

Barbaric Vast & Wild: A Gathering of Outside and
Subterranean Poetry (*Poems for the Millennium*, vol. 5).
Jerome Rothenberg and John Bloomberg-Rissman,
editors.

Clayton Eshleman: The Whole Art by Stuart Kendall

Revolution of the Mind: The Life of André Breton
by Mark Polizzotti